Genre Myth

Essential Question

Why do people tell and retell myths?

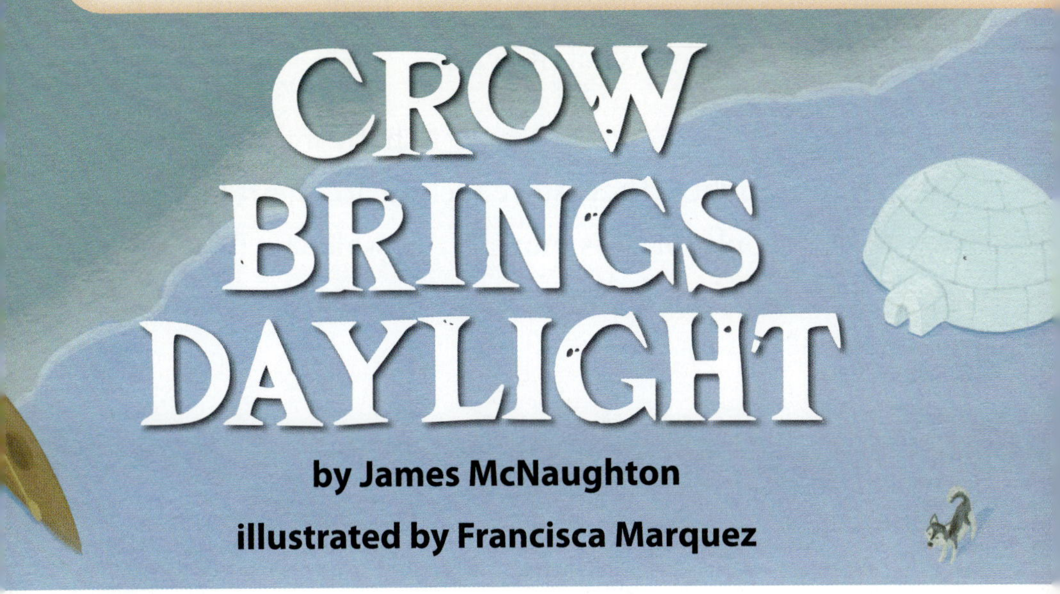

CROW BRINGS DAYLIGHT

by James McNaughton

illustrated by Francisca Marquez

CHAPTER 1

DARKNESS IN THE NORTH

Many years ago, the Inuit people of the far north lived in darkness. They had never seen the sun. They did not even know what it was.

The people had to hunt and fish by moonlight. On the darkest nights, they stayed close to their homes. For these people, it was normal to wake up in the dark. The **somber** light of their torches did not seem gloomy or sad to them.

When the people needed food, they gathered around holes in the ice to fish. They needed their dogs to warn them of bears or other dangers because they could not see very far.

One night, an old crow returned from a long journey. There was a full moon, so the people were outside enjoying its pale light. Crow sighed when he saw how happy the moonlight made the people.

An old man was walking past with his grandsons. "Hello, Crow," he said. "Why are you sighing?"

"I have just come from the south, where there is something called daylight," Crow said. "Daylight is far brighter than moonlight, and it fills the sky with warmth and color. Now that I have seen daylight, the far north seems very cold and **desolate**."

"Crow, you're even older than I am," the old man said. "I have heard about your many adventures. With so many **exploits**, why do you make up silly stories?"

Crow insisted that he was telling the truth, but the old man didn't believe him.

However, the old man's grandsons wanted to hear more. As soon as they could, they said good-bye to their grandfather and hurried back to Crow.

Crow began to tell the boys about daylight. Before long, a crowd of young people had gathered to listen and ask questions. Then the children's parents came over. Some left quickly because they did not believe Crow, but others stayed.

The old man saw what was happening. He waved his arms to **shoo** Crow away and shouted, "Stop telling lies!"

The old man chased Crow to the other end of the village. Some villagers continued to talk about daylight. They were excited and wished they could see it for themselves.

Crow was resting at the edge of the village when the people came to find him. He thought they might be angry, but then he saw that they were smiling.

"Crow, we want you to fly south and bring daylight back to us," one of the old man's grandsons said. Many other people added words of **encouragement**, telling Crow that they were sure he could do it.

Crow was happy that the people believed him, but he did not want to take another long journey. "The south is very far away," he said, "and I'm old."

The villagers begged him to go because there was no one else who could do it.

"All right, I'll go," Crow said finally. "But I won't be back for a long time."

STOP AND CHECK

Why do the villagers want Crow to fly south?

CHAPTER 2

CROW SETS OUT

The people cheered as Crow flew up into the sky. Their burning torches became smaller and then disappeared from view as he headed south. Now all he could see was complete darkness. It didn't even matter if his eyes were open or closed. Crow felt lonely and afraid, and he was already tired. The cheers of the people had given him energy, but that energy had faded along with the torches.

However, Crow was **steadfast** and would not let anything stop him from reaching the south. His instincts told him which way to go. He could not see or hear anything, and he did not know how much time had passed. All he knew was that he was very tired.

Crow flew on and on in the darkness. He was about to let himself slow down and rest when he saw light in the distance.

The light grew brighter and brighter as Crow flew toward it. Little by little, he was able to see the forest beneath him. Soon the whole sky was bright, and he could see clearly for miles. The trees below were covered with **sparkling** snow that glittered and glowed in the sunlight. He could see the huge, blue ocean and the white waves crashing on its shore.

Crow felt the warmth of the sun and was filled with relief. He had made it to the south. He stopped flapping his wings and began a slow **descent** down to the ground.

Crow landed in a tree by a river. As he hopped onto a branch, he made clumps of snow drop to the ground like little snowballs. Then he found a sunny spot and rested. He felt exhausted but happy. The water in the river leaped and danced in the light. "You made it, old Crow," the river seemed to sing.

A beautiful young woman came down to the river to get water. The woman's black hair was shining in the sun. "People look better in daylight," Crow thought. He turned himself into a speck of dust and drifted down onto the woman's coat.

She carried him to a village and went into a wooden house. It was the home of the village chief.

STOP AND CHECK

Why does Crow think people look better in daylight?

CHAPTER 3

A SMALL BALL OF LIGHT

The house was warm and cozy. The chief was carving a fishhook out of wood, and his little grandson was playing on the floor.

Crow saw a box at the back of the room. Light glowed brightly from under its lid. Crow knew that he had found daylight.

The young woman took off her coat. Crow was still a speck of dust. He fell off the coat and into the little boy's ear. The boy **immediately** sat up and started crying right away.

The chief put down his carving and picked up the boy. "What's wrong, little man?" he asked.

Crow whispered in the boy's ear, "Say 'I want a ball of daylight.'"

The boy repeated Crow's words.

"Daughter, did you hear that?" the chief said to the woman. "He wants a ball of daylight. What a clever boy! Will you bring me the box, please?"

The boy's mother carefully carried the box to the chief. The chief opened the lid, took out a ball of daylight, and held it out to the boy.

The boy was too frightened to touch the glowing ball, so the chief tied a piece of string around it. "Just hold on to the string," he said, handing it to the boy.

The boy took the string and pulled on it, which made the glowing ball jump. Soon he was swinging the ball in circles, enjoying how the light and shadow danced on the walls.

Crow scratched the inside of the boy's ear. "Say 'I want to play outside,'" he whispered.

Once again, the boy repeated Crow's words.

The chief helped the boy put on his coat and carried him outside. Just then, the speck of dust fell out of the boy's ear and turned into Crow. Crow grabbed the ball of daylight with his claws and flew up into the air. The boy **wailed** and cried, and the furious chief shouted at Crow.

Soon Crow couldn't hear them as he flew high over the forest, heading back to the far north.

STOP AND CHECK

How does turning into a speck of dust help Crow steal daylight?

CHAPTER 4

LIGHT IN THE NORTH

So much time had passed that many people in the far north had forgotten about Crow. Only the old man's grandsons still believed that Crow would return.

"You are foolish to wait," their grandfather said. "Crow is too ashamed of his **deception** to return. He should not have had the **audacity** to tell such lies."

The boys went outside before their grandfather could continue his lecture. There, they noticed a bright star that seemed to be moving closer. The boys were frightened and called for help.

The villagers rushed out of their igloos and watched as the star grew larger and brighter. When the people saw Crow carrying the bright light, they began to cheer.

Crow dropped the ball onto the ice, where it broke open and let out daylight. The world lit up with color, and the ice and snow sparkled. The people began to laugh and cry with happiness.

Crow landed in a pile of snow, and the people gathered around to thank him. They said their lives would be much better with daylight. They would be able to hunt and fish all the time instead of only when the moon was bright.

Someone noticed that the air was getting warmer. They all unbuttoned their coats and thanked Crow for the warmth, too. They thanked him again and again, saying that everything in their lives would be better.

Finally, Crow had rested enough to speak. He said, "I brought only one ball of daylight. It is small and will burn out in six months. It will then take six months to **recharge** its energy. While the ball gets its energy back, the land will be in darkness for half of the year."

"We're used to darkness," the people told Crow. "We're grateful to have any light at all."

The grandfather knelt down in the snow beside Crow. "I'm sorry I doubted you," he said. "You are very **valiant**. You have helped us more than I can say. I was **oblivious** to how much better things could be. Now I am much more aware."

From that day on, the Inuit have always been kind to Crow because he brought them the gift of daylight.

STOP AND CHECK

Why don't the people mind having daylight for only half of the year?

Respond to Reading

Summarize

Use details from the story to summarize *Crow Brings Daylight*. Your graphic organizer may help you.

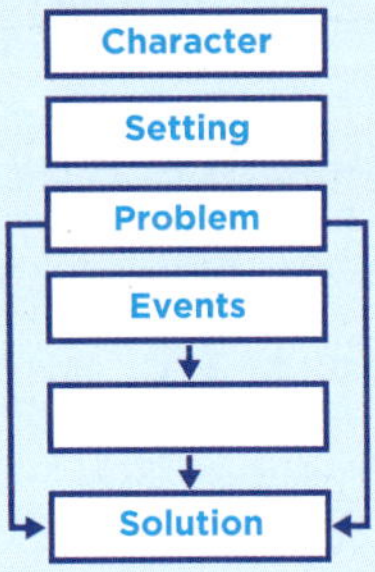

Text Evidence

1. How does Crow take the daylight?
   PROBLEM AND SOLUTION

2. Find the word *clumps* on page 8. What clues help you to understand the word's meaning?
   VOCABULARY

3. Write about the problems that Crow solved for the people of the far north. **WRITE ABOUT READING**

Genre Parody

Compare Texts

Read an updated version of the myth about Crow and daylight.

Crow Retires

Old Crow landed with a thump on top of an igloo. A man came out of the igloo and greeted the exhausted bird. "Where have you been, Crow?" he asked.

"I've been in the south," Crow said. "I didn't like it. They have something called daylight, which is brighter than a thousand full moons."

The man thought that daylight sounded wonderful, but Crow insisted that the man was wrong.

"Darkness is better," Crow said. "My wrinkles don't show, and it matches the color of my feathers. I have come back to the far north to retire."

The man wanted to hear more about daylight, but Crow said he needed to rest.

The man thought about daylight for a long time. He decided that it would be a very good thing. Finally, he asked Crow to go get daylight and bring it back to the far north.

Crow told the man to go and get it himself, but the man did not leave him alone. Soon all the people were begging Crow to go get daylight. He tried to tell them that they would not like it, but they didn't believe him.

"You'll have to clean more because dirt will show in the daylight," he said.

But the people were sure that daylight would make their lives better. They bothered Crow so much that he finally agreed to go, just to get away from them.

Crow flew up into the air and headed south.

When Crow arrived in the south, he rested in a tree by a river. He looked around and realized that he had missed the colors and the warmth of the sun. A beautiful young woman came down to the river to get some water. She ignored him, which made him happy. Maybe the people here would leave him alone.

"It's so peaceful here," Crow said to himself. "And it would take me such a long time to fly back to the far north."

Crow did not like the idea of returning to the dark north. He decided to stay in the south to retire.

So Crow stayed in the tree as much as possible and had a long and happy retirement in the sunny south.

Make Connections

How could updating a myth lead to people telling it more? **ESSENTIAL QUESTION**

Compare the endings in *Crow Brings Daylight* and *Crow Retires*. How are they different? **TEXT TO TEXT**

Focus on Genre

Myth Myths are a form of folk stories. They usually tell about gods or heroic figures. Sometimes they explain things that happen in the natural world. Myths come from many different cultures. They often have characters with supernatural powers. They usually take place long ago, when the world was different from how it is today.

Read and Find In *Crow Brings Daylight*, Crow has powers that real birds don't have. Crow is a bird that can talk with humans and change into a speck of dust.

Your Turn

Work with a partner or small group. Reread *Crow Brings Daylight*. Discuss the following questions.

Who is a hero in this myth? What clues can you find about a character who meets a challenge or keeps a promise?

How is the setting of this myth different from the world today?

What yearly events in the natural world does this myth explain?